Lies That
Tell the Truth

Lies That
Tell the Truth

A BOOK OF AND ABOUT METAPHOR

Carolyn Pinkard

Writer's Showcase
San Jose   New York   Lincoln   Shanghai

Lies That Tell the Truth

Writer's Showcase
an imprint of iUniverse.com, Inc.

For information address:
iUniverse.com, Inc.
5220 S 16th, Ste. 200
Lincoln, NE 68512
www.iuniverse.com

ISBN: 0-595-15866-8

Printed in the United States of America

For my parents

Elsie Karlsson Aronson

Melcher Mortimer Aronson

ACKNOWLEDGMENTS

When my friends learned that I was writing a book about metaphors, they were quick to offer encouragement and favorite metaphors of their own. I am grateful to them for both gifts.

Very special thanks go to members of my family:

— to my son Eric who made up for my lack of computer literacy by typing the manuscript of this book.

— to my husband, Calvin, who not only critiqued my writing but whisked me off to dinner or other distraction when I was stuck overlong on getting something said in the best and clearest way.

— to my young grandchildren, Ben and Carrie, who speak in metaphors without conscious effort, and who patiently repeated them when I asked so I could write them down.

And last, I want to thank all those who have created metaphors. These authors are legion, and the metaphors they wrote a treasure trove for all of us.

TABLE OF CONTENTS

FOREWORD

For years I have copied passages I like from the reading I do. Up to now I have filled several of those handy blank books that bookstores sell with these excerpts. About a year ago on rereading my collection I noticed how many of my favorite passages are metaphors. That's when this book was born.

I decided then to write an article about metaphor: what it *is*, what it *does*. When my notes became too many, and my thoughts too long, I decided to write a book—this book.

I wrote it for those who have little technical knowledge of metaphor and no particular urge to acquire it. Instead I wanted to bring to the reader of this book knowledge of how to recognize the metaphors they read and hear. I wanted also to give suggestions for ways to analyze a metaphor in order to appreciate all it has to tell.

A Supreme Court justice once wrote (in an opinion on a case about pornography) "I can't tell you exactly what pornography is, but I know it when I see it." On finishing this book I hope the reader will have the same confident ability to recognize metaphor. And I hope, having identified a metaphor, he/she will know how to discover the riches in it.

C.P.

Lies That
Tell the Truth

Metaphor offers me new visions
of experience, in language
that astonishes my soul,
transforming words into
life and life into words
wreathed with grace and
weighted with intensity.

JUDITH VIORST

What Metaphor *Is*

In Eden, as the myth says, Adam named every living thing. Imagine him, so very unpracticed in using words as he must have been, struggling with this immense task, and learning gradually as he went along, the power there is in words. And ever since, history reveals, men have tried to fashion language that has power. In each generation there arises again the belief that if we can just get language right so very much will eventually follow.

Metaphor has been one of the brilliant successes in the effort to discover words with power. Indeed, the language of men in all ages is shot through with metaphor. It shines from the earliest recorded poetry and from the poetry of all later societies. Story and novel and essay and biography contain metaphor. It enlivened the speeches of orators of the past. In our time politicians, sports announcers, and those who try to tell us what's going on in the stock market stud their speeches with metaphor. (In the case of the latter their whole analysis of doings on Wall Street is apt to be nothing *but* metaphor) For teachers and preachers metaphor is the coin of realm. "Ordinary" people have always used metaphor and, of course, still do.

What, then is metaphor which blossoms in so many environments, common as daisies? In truth, most of us don't know exactly what metaphor is, or have only a dim memory of something taught long ago in some classroom.

We need to learn much more of metaphor if we are to appreciate what it is and what it does.

Aristotle once said that all attempts to define anything, to say in words what anything *is*, are useless. He urged the study of examples of a thing as the only fruitful method for coming to know its true nature. Aristotle's advice is taken seriously in this book. There are many examples of metaphor in it because I, too, believe that examples yield a deeper and fuller understanding of what metaphor is than definitions of it framed in words.

Nevertheless, we begin with definitions made in words. They offer, not full-blooded metaphor, but something like an architect's drawing that shows the underlying structure of a building. They can give a start toward understanding metaphor.

A dictionary usually begins a definition of a thing by naming the category into which it falls. (A bear is an animal.) This narrows things but doesn't tell us, for instance, how to tell a bear from a camel. The dictionary then adds important distinguishing features of the thing being defined. (A bear is one of a family of large quadrupeds having long, shaggy fur and a five-toed foot.) That specific information is of more help in knowing a bear when we see one but it is limited to factual description. It tells nothing of what, say, a hunter knows of a bear, or a bear knows of a bear, or bear cubs know of their mother although these intangibles are as important as facts are in knowing the totality of *bear*.

So it is with metaphor. A metaphor may be defined as a verbal expression but that definition-by-a-category does not single out metaphor from question, or phrase, or exclamation. But adding that a metaphor is a *figurative* expression, or, as linguists say, *a figure of speech*, is a more explicit definition of what a metaphor is.

Any instance of figurative language makes a statement that is not factual, not literally true in a physical world of space and time and objects that are and can be counted on to remain different from each other. (A chair will not be a piece of pie the next time you approach it.)

Here is an example of figurative language.

Henry is the rotten apple in the basket.

It seems unnecessary to say (but it is necessary here) that Henry is no kind of apple. The statement that he *is* a decayed fruit is nonliteral, logically impossible, irrational, a lie. But if we recognize that this characterization of Henry is figurative language it makes sense to us. It makes the kind of meaningful but not literal truth that metaphor makes. A definition by Jack Niles puts it like this:

> When none of the "right ways"
> of saying a thing is adequate,
> we choose a "wrong way" so as
> to have access into some deeper rightness.

A way that many language experts define metaphor is to call it a comparison between two unlike things. One such definition reads:

> A metaphor points to correspondence between two things usually thought of as unlike.
>
> FROM *The Poets Dictionary*

Here an example of a metaphor that fits the definition will be helpful. It consists of a brief—and famous—speech by Hamlet in Shakespeare's play.

> Death is that undiscovered country from whose bourne (realm) no traveler returns.

In this metaphor Hamlet likens death to a certain kind of country. Without doubt it compares two things we regard as not at all alike. But note too that the comparison is radical. The metaphor actually claims that death and a country of a certain kind are *identical.*

The claim of identity outrages logic. In rational thought two distinct things cannot be the same thing. (The world gets very shaky if one cannot tell a dead person from a country.) Yet the reader of Hamlet's metaphor knows what it means and will not discard his words because what they say is not literally what they mean. To paraphrase: There is more in the world, Horatio, than all your logical systems know.

Another significant definition of metaphor is made in this statement by Robert Alter.

> A metaphor is powerful language because it has the ability to break open closed frames of reference and makes us see things with a shock of new recognition.

This definition by a noted critic of poetry focuses on how the reader is affected by the powerful language of metaphor. The effect, Alter says, is nothing less than a radical change in how the reader perceives some part of the physical world or the world of spirit.

Notoriously, with age and accumulated experience, human beings perceive as they have been taught to perceive, as they have become accustomed to see and hear and even taste.

There is stability in this and risk diminishes. On the flip side there is self-inflicted boredom spawned by sameness.

In Alter's definition metaphor is an instrument that shatters ways of perceiving and understanding by forcing new views of things and people and ideas on the reader. In this definition the reaction to metaphor is insight.

Closely allied with the thrust of Alter's definition of metaphor as a force that breaks up the old and monotonous is another that makes a similar point:

> A metaphor is a journey away from the humdrum to seeing new relationships.

New Oxford Guide to Writing

There are other definitions of metaphor. In fact there are quite a number of them. During a day spent delving into volumes in a university library I found twenty eight of them. In these definitions there was overlap but not too much. Probably this is to be expected in the case of any multifaceted thing. One definition emphasizes one or two facets, another, other features.

Among the definitions I found was one which suggested that the author had tried to put all he knew about metaphor into one definition. The author was a don at Oxford in the 1800's and the definition appears as a conclusion to a long scholarly essay he wrote on metaphor. I imagine him in his university digs, wearing his long gown, and occasionally glancing through a gothic window at the quad, as he composed this:

> In metaphor one thing, idea, action, person, is referred to by a word or expression normally denoting another thing so as to suggest a common quality possessed by the two. It is a figure of speech that by peculiar phrasing embodies a perception previously outside the perceptual realm of the reader of the metaphor.

The don, perhaps, was proud of his scholarship and satisfied with his detailed description of metaphor. I admire his ability to control two lengthy sentences but I find the definition itself just the opposite of metaphor which is almost invariably concise, colorful, and easy to remember.

So I offer for this book a definition for metaphor adopted from Plato who proposed it as a definition of myth.

A metaphor is a lie that tells the truth.

Plato, great philosopher and myth maker of Ancient Greece, said of myth that it tells a story purportedly true but actually false. His own famous *Myth of the Cave* recounts that men were fastened to the walls of a cave in such a way that they could not see out of it. Their heads were fixed in a position that permitted them to see only straight ahead at the walls of the cave. There they could see only shadows created by fires built behind them. In this way the men who tended the fires could govern what the prisoners saw. Over time the men became convinced that the shadow figures made up all the content of the world. They became sure that the shadows they saw were the only reality. Plato acknowledged that the cave incident never happened as historical event. It was no more true than that Hercules performed his prodigious labors or that Prometheus stole fire from the gods.

While not true in themselves, myths did tell a truth according to Plato. The cave myth tells, in symbolic fashion, how men create their own reality and mistake it for the only reality. This, for Plato was the reason for myth—it teaches a moral or ethical truth by means of a story any one can follow and almost certainly will because the teller of a myth can count on man's inborn craving for narrative. Plato believed, also, that all educators have a moral obligation to teach. But not everyone can learn philosophy when phrased in the abstract and, for many, difficult language used by philosophers. With many, perhaps most people, the myth offers the ideal teaching method because it is short, vividly expressed and easily remembered. Moreover it points to a truth that will influence the belief and so the behavior of the hearer.

In a sense a metaphor resembles a myth in miniature although it has no more than the seed of a narrative element. It tells a lie (Henry is not a rotten apple. Death is not a country.) but the lie is a means for telling a truth. It too is concise, expressed in vivid language, and influences how the one who reads it or hears it sees the world and what goes on in it.

A lie that tells the truth as definition of a metaphor is also easily remembered. In reaching understanding of the examples of metaphor in this book the definition can be used like a microscope to detect the lie in any metaphor and then with more powerful lens the underlying truth.

How great is the debt
owed to metaphor
by those who, knowing
what they want to say,
wish to illumine and
vivify it.

H. W. FOWLER

Kinds of Metaphor

Is Metaphor

Although words are the "ingredients" of all metaphors, one kind of metaphor differs from another in how the words are arranged. That is, each kind of metaphor has a unique word-pattern.

The *is* metaphor word pattern can be seen in this metaphor:

> Today, gold is God.
>
> Eugene Debs

The word pattern is:
  Noun (gold)
  Verb (is, a form of the verb, to be)
  another Noun (God)

Today is important to the meaning of the metaphor but is not part of the *noun-verb-noun* basic pattern.

Any *is* metaphor, too, follows a pattern which can be expressed as:

> *This is That*

And if you're mathematically-minded the pattern

$$A=B$$

will do. Take your choice of pattern. They are equivalents. Each represents an *is* metaphor stripped to the bone. Each claims an identity between two *different* things, usually two *very* different things. Knowing the basic pattern of *is* metaphor provides the means to ferret out the basic metaphor from among the other words in the sentence containing the metaphor. Once you have done this, you will find that the other words qualify the *is* metaphor in important ways. Finding the basic *is* metaphor, then finding how the other words qualify it, is the best way to go in order to comprehend all that an *is* metaphor has to say.

Of course, you may not have to know the word-pattern of an *is* metaphor in order to understand it. Sometimes *is* metaphor (or any kind of metaphor) jumps out of the page at you just as a white figure stands out against a black background. You know, it seems instantly (although numerous unconscious processes of mind occur to produce the result), what the metaphor means. This is all to the good, and you may have had this reaction to *Today, gold is God*. But if, recognizing at once that a statement *is* a metaphor, the reader pauses to explore the metaphor further he/she is likely to plumb its depths more deeply.

One way to explore an *is* metaphor beyond a first impression of its meaning, requires questioning it. For instance, some of the questions I would ask of our example of *is* metaphor are:

How are gold and God alike despite their obvious differences?

How do I, and others, behave similarly toward God and gold?

Is the value a society assigns to gold at all like the value it assigns to God?

Are gold and God like each other in physical characteristics, function, status in society?

There is no set of standard questions to ask of any *is* metaphor. The questions necessarily will depend upon the content of the metaphor itself. Questions will come to your mind as you explore any *is* metaphor, more so as you become practiced in questioning. In the end the answers to your questions will bring out the underlying truth beneath the superficial lie the metaphor tells.

A suggestion: It is not necessary to be overly serious and earnest in questioning a metaphor. Giving your imagination free play in framing questions and listening to the answers your imagination supplies will prove to be very productive and fun too. You might also devise an imaginary dialogue between the *This* and *That* of any *is* metaphor. What you do is to take the role of each in turn. Let them speak freely to each other. A good place to begin is to have each say to the other what they like and dislike about being called the same as the other. You are likely to find that out of this sort of imaginary dialogue a deeper understanding of the metaphor will arise.

Here are some *is* metaphors. I begin with brief ones and go on to others in which the basic structure must be identified before you can work with them.

Happiness is a warm puppy.

Lucy from the Peanuts comic strip

Architecture is frozen music.

Friedrich von Schelling

To a thirsty throat, cold water is good news from a distant land.

from *Proverbs*

Work is the scourge of the drinking classes.

OSCAR WILDE

The sky is the daily bread of the eyes.

RALPH WALDO EMERSON

But soft! What light through yonder window breaks? It is the east and Juliet is the sun.

WILLIAM SHAKESPEARE

Religion is the sign of the distressed creature, the heart of the heartless world…it is the opium of the people.

KARL MARX

*(There are three **is** metaphors in these words of Karl Marx. The last is the most famous—and controversial.)*

I am no man, I am dynamite.

FRIEDRICH NIETZSCHE

Science pronounces only on whatever, at the time, appears to have been scientifically ascertained, which is a small island in an ocean of ignorance.

BERTRAND RUSSELL

(Professor Ellis, an authority on Thomas Jefferson, not noted for idolizing this president of the United States, told the following story on a C Span program.)

Professor Ellis: At the end of a lecture I gave on Jefferson, I asked for comments from the audience. An elderly woman who, in appearance, seemed to be the epitome of a sweet little old lady rose to her feet and said, "It is a disgrace, young man, that you spoke of Thomas Jefferson as you did. Why, your speech was nothing but bird droppings on a noble statue of that great man."

While walking along in a black forest carrying a lantern, someone comes along and tells you to blow out *your* lantern and follow him and *his* lantern.

That man is a theologian.

DIDEROT

(The following are words attributed to Socrates as he defended himself against the charge of corrupting the youth of Athens. His accusers have demanded the death penalty. He responded to them thus:)

"…if you kill me you will not easily find a successor to me who am a gadfly, and the state is a great and noble steed who is tardy in his motions owing to his very size, and requires to be stirred into life. I am that gadfly…and all day long am always fastening on you, arousing you."

Verb as Metaphor

Metaphor always expresses a comparison between two things usually perceived as being distinctly different. But various grammatical structures can be used to convey metaphor. The simplest of these structures I call *metaphor-in-a-verb* for the metaphor consists solely of any form (past, present, future, participle, infinitive, etc.) of a verb. "The ship *plowed* the sea." This metaphor-in-a-verb was created over two thousand years ago by the great poet, Homer, a master of metaphor. To understand how a metaphor is conveyed by the verb *plowed* in Homer's sentence, one must use his/her imagination. Specifically one must bring to mind's eye a picture of a plow moving across a field. Attending to this picture shows how a plow, moving through the earth, throws dirt to each side as it moves in a steady pace across a field.

Now, in the same way, imagine an ancient ship moving across the Mediterranean Sea, its prow partly submerged in water and throwing water to each side as it moves along toward its destination. Last, place the two images side by side as is done when splitscreen images appear side by side on a TV. When you compare the two images on the split screen of your mind, the similarity between the action of the ship and the action of the plow becomes obvious. We see that Homer has chosen a verb that makes an apt comparison.

I have suggested that making images in your mind is essential to understanding metaphor-in-a-verb. I know that some readers will doubt they are up to the task of seeing images in their mind's eye. When I worked as a psychotherapist I met many people with this conviction. I asked them to close their eyes, then imagine a home they lived in as a child, then to walk about (in imagination) in this home describing what they saw. I asked, for example, how many windows there were in their former home and how many doors. Also I asked each one to find a favorite toy, or pet in their childhood home and describe it. Almost anyone can do this exercise and the ability to do it is proof of the capacity to image. Indeed, this capacity is inherent in humans and is essential to many of their activities. One of these activities is understanding and fully appreciating any metaphor-in-a-verb. There follows examples of metaphors-in-a-verb. In each case the verb-metaphor is italicized.

They (sailors) sprang to orders, hoisting the pinewood mast, they stepped it firm in its block amidships, lashed it fast and with braided rawhide halyards hauled the white sail high. Suddenly, wind hit full and the canvas *bellied out*.

(To fully appreciate this metaphor place on your mind screen, side by side, a sail suddenly catching a high wind and the belly of an obese person protruding from his body.)

> Among the words *outlawed* in speeches delivered in the House of Commons of the British Parliament are blackguard, cad, hypocrite, slander, villain…
>
> FROM AN ARTICLE IN *THE NEW YORK TIMES*

> I urge a 16th Amendment (to the U.S. Constitution) because mankind suffrage is civil, religious and social disorganization. The male element is a destructive force, stern, selfish, aggrandizing, loving war, violence, conquest, acquisition, *breeding* in the material and moral world alike, discord, disorder, disease and death.
>
> ELIZABETH CODY STANTON FROM A SPEECH ADVOCATING WOMEN'S SUFFRAGE

> We died; is that enough?
> Many died well of both sides;

Most of us died uselessly.
But never use our murdered days
To garnish your tomorrow.

JAMES AGEE FROM THE POEM *WE SOLDIERS OF ALL NATIONS*

(England) has sent us swarms of officials who *eat* our people's substance.

THOMAS JEFFERSON IN THE *DECLARATION OF INDEPENDENCE*

(In a very few words, by alluding to swarming locusts, Jefferson compares the activities of the many English officials foisted on the American colonies by England to the destruction locusts cause by eating crops.)

Statesmen and historians have long known that a common enemy is the most solidifying thing a nation can have, *welding* all the people into a united front. No wonder a dictator, when he feels uneasy, looks for something for his people to squash.

E. B. WHITE

How doth the city *sit* solitary, that was full of people. How is she become a widow! She that was great among nations, and princess among provinces, how she is become tributary.

JEREMIAH

*(Note how, using a metaphor-in-a-verb and several **is-metaphors,** Jeremiah movingly describes how a city is utterly changed.)*

O lord…
I seek you but you don't heed,
Not knowing you *hold the reins*
Of my soul, my life.

ANACREAN

You, yourselves have seen what I did in Egypt. *I bore you upon eagles' wings* and brought you unto me.

MOSES

(The above is one of the best known metaphors of the Hebrew Bible. It is a part of what many biblical scholars call The Eagle Speech. *The first sentence refers to the punishing acts of god, YHVH, directed toward the Egyptians who held His people captive in Egypt treating them like slaves and refusing to let them leave. By contrast, the second sentence refers to YHVH's tender care as He guided the people on their trek from Egypt to the Mountain of God. It was from this mountain that Moses delivered* The Eagle Speech. *In it he compares the loving care YHVH shows for His people to the action of an eagle toward his nestlings when they are ready to learn to fly. At this point in their lives the nestlings are fearful of flying on their own. The great eagle then lifts up one of the eaglets, drops it on one of his great wings and flies off moving slowly and then at a faster pace as he gyrates in the air. At length the eaglet dares to flex it's own wings. There could scarcely be a more apt comparison between the way that the eagle bears his young in flight and the way that a god encourages, instructs, and loves a community of fearful former slaves as they journey toward the unknown.*

Another feature of the eagle metaphor can be noted. It would have been easily understood by people who had many opportunities to observe eagles so that eagle behavior was well known to them. In the United States today, most of us have few or no opportunities to observe eagles in the wild. To understand the eagle metaphor made by Moses we need information about a world different from ours.)

Metaphor in Analogy

Allegory, myth, parable, fable, legend—all are a form of analogy. All, too, bear the identifying marks of metaphor: each suggests similarity between things or ideas or situations that are different; each tells a lie that tells the truth.

Further, these kinds of analogy all tell a story, a story that could be enjoyed for its own sake. But the purpose of these analogic stories is not just to amuse readers. Much more, the aim of these stories is to convey truth, teach a lesson, suggest what relations between human and human, and god and human *should* be.

The authors of the stories take advantage of the love of narrative that is inbred in humans. In making these stories, century after century, their authors attest to a conviction that stories, far more than abstractions will be understood and remembered.

In the tales that follow, you need not hunt for the lie. The lie is the story itself. It is obvious, at least to the modern adult mind, that when a story is about the actions of imperious and immortal gods, animals who can talk and who have the emotions of men, or who are half god-half man, or fabulous creatures with one eye, or rocks in the sea that seduce and swallow men, or a giant, or a witch, that story is not literally true.

Nonetheless, after reading such a nonfactual story, you can read it again searching for the truth it tells.

Sometimes, you may know immediately the truth the story has conveyed. But, when insight does not come at once, you must think about what the underlying message is, checking back and forth between story and dawning idea until insight comes. Most of the stories that follow have been told over and over again during a long period of time. This suggests they have been found valuable by many readers and to many teachers. It suggests, also, that the stories deal with issues that matter to human beings.

Your experience with the stories that follow will tell you more about the nature of metaphor and the nature of life.

THE EWE LAMB

Two men in the same city, one rich and one poor. The rich man had very large flocks and herds, but the poor man had only one little ewe lamb that he had bought. He tended it and it grew up together with him and his children: it used to share his morsel of bread, drink from his cup, and nestle in his bosom; it was like a daughter to him. One day a traveler came to the rich man, but he was loath to take anything from his own flocks or herds to prepare a meal for the guest who had come to him: so he took the poor man's lamb and prepared it for the man who had come to him.

David flew into a rage against the man and said to Nathan, "As the Lord lives, the man who did this deserves to die! He shall pay for the lamb four times over, because he did such a thing and showed no pity." And Nathan said to David, "That man is you!"

(Perhaps wanting to be sure that David gets the metaphor, Nathan gives him a broad hint. Usually explaining a metaphor is as bad as explaining a joke but in this instance the hint pointed David in the direction of insight into himself and the meaning of his own behavior.)

THE GOOD SAMARITAN

Once a certain scribe stood up and said, "Rabbi, what must I do to gain eternal life?" And Jesus said to him, "What is written in the Law?"

And the scribe said, "You shall love the Lord your God with all your heart and with all your soul and with all your strength and with all your mind, and you shall love your neighbor as yourself."

And Jesus said, "You have answered correctly. Do this and you will live."

And the scribe said, "But who is my neighbor?"

And Jesus said, "A certain man while traveling from Jerusalem to Jericho, was set upon by robbers, who stripped him and beat him, and left him on the road, half dead. And a priest happened to be going down that road and when he saw him, he passed by on the other side. And a Levite, too, came to that place and saw him and passed by on the other side. But a Samaritan who was traveling that way came upon the man, and when he saw him, he was moved with compassion, and he went over to him and bound up his wounds pouring oil and wine on them, and put him on his own donkey and brought him to an inn and took care of him. And on the next day he took out two silver coins and gave them to the innkeeper and said, "Take care of him; and if it costs more than this, I will reimburse you when I come back.

Which of these three, do you think, turned out to be a neighbor to that man?

And the scribe said, "The one who treated him with mercy."

And Jesus said, "Go then and do as he did."

THE YOUNG MAN AND THE SWALLOW
(A fable of Aesop)

A prodigal young spendthrift, who had wasted his whole patrimony in taverns and gaming houses among lewd, idle company, was taking a melancholy walk near a brook. It was in the month of January, and happened to be one of those warm, sunshiny days which sometimes smile upon us even in that wintry season of the year. A swallow, which had made his appearance by mistake too soon, flew along the surface of the water. The giddy youth, observing this, concluded that summer was come, and that he should have little or no occasion for clothes, so he went and pawned them, and ventured the money for one stake more among his sharping companions. When this too was gone the same way with the rest, he took another solitary walk in the same place as before. But the weather, being severe and frosty, had made everything look with an aspect very different from what it did before: the brook was quite frozen over, and the poor swallow lay dead upon the bank of it...Whereupon the young man reproached the deceased bird as the author of all his misfortunes, "Ah, wretch that thou wert!" says he, "Thou hast undone me."

WHAT IS AN ELEPHANT?

On one occasion a number of disciples went to the Blessed One and said, "Sir, there are living here in Savatthi many wandering hermits and scholars who indulge in constant dispute.... What, Sir, would you say concerning them?"

The Blessed One answered, "Brethren, those disputatious fellows are like unto blind men..."

"Once upon a time there was a rajah in this region who called to a certain man and said, 'gather together in one place all the men in Savatthi who were born blind and show them an elephant.'

"Very good sire,' said the man, and did what he was told, and said to them, 'O Blind, such as this is an elephant!—and to one man he presented the head of an elephant, to another its ears, to another a tusk, to another the trunk, the foot, back, tail and tuft of the tail, saying to each one that that was the elephant.'"

Thereupon, brethren, that rajah went up to the blind men and said to each, "Tell me what sort of thing is an elephant?"

Thereupon those who had been presented with the head answered, 'Sire, an elephant is like a pot,' And those that observed an ear only replied, 'An elephant is like a winnowing basket,' Those who had been presented with a tusk said the body was granary; the foot, a pillar; the back, a mortar; the tail, a pestle; the tuft of the tail, just a broom.

Then they began to quarrel shouting 'Yes it is!' 'No, it isnt.' 'An elephant is not like that.' And so on until they came to fisticuffs over the matter. Then, brethren, that rajah was delighted with the scene. Just so are these wanderers holding other views, blind, unseeing, knowing not the unprofitable, knowing not the profitable. They know not the Law. They know not what is not the Law. In their ignorance of these things they are quarrelsome, wrangling and vastly disputatious, each maintaining it is thus and thus."

UDANA IV A BOOK OF BUDDHIST WISDOM

NASRUDIN

The four tales that follow are to be found in The Pleasantries of the Incredible Mulla, Nasrudin. *The author is Idries Shah, a Muslim scholar who claimed (with tongue in cheek) to have heard them told by a rural Mulla, a sort of wise man and counselor to a village of peasants. The stories are in the tradition of Sufi (a Muslim sect) teaching stories. The tales are, in essence, absurdities that tell the truth.*

FIXED IDEAS

'How old are you, Mulla?'
'Forty.'
'But you said the same the last time I asked you.'
'Yes, I always stand by what I have said.'

WE COME AND WE GO

'Where do we come from and where do we go to, and what is it like?' thundered a wandering dervish.
'I don't know,' said Nasrudin; but it must be pretty terrible.'
A bystander asked him why.

'Observation shows me that when we arrive as babies we are crying. And many of us leave crying, and reluctantly too.'

WHICH WAY ROUND

A man who had studied at many metaphysical schools came to Nasrudin: In order to show that he could be accepted for discipleship he described in detail where he had been and what he had studied.

'I hope you will accept me, or at least tell me your ideas,' he said, 'because I have spent so much of my time in studying at these schools.'

'Alas!' said Nasrudin, '*You* have studied the teachers and their teachings. What should have happened is that the teachers should have studied *you*. Then we would have had something worthwhile.'

TRY ANYTHING ONCE

Nasrudin was lurking near a tavern. He was penniless: and besides wine was forbidden to true believers. The sultan's cup-bearer came out, carefully carrying a delicate flagon of wine.

They caught sight of one another at the same moment.

'Honourable Saki,' began the Mulla, 'give me—'

Give you *what*, Mulla?

To ask for wine would be a direct admission that he drank it.

'Give me—a piece of advice.'

'Very well. Go and read a book.'

Half to himself, Nasrudin muttered: 'Oh no, that won't do.'

'Why not?'

'Oh…er…I tried that once.'

THE MYTH OF SISYPHUS

Sisyphus, a mortal, lived by thieving. He was known everywhere for his cleverness and audacity. But he overreached himself in telling the river god Asopus where Zeus had hidden his daughter Aegina after Zeus abducted her. Because Sisyphus gave Asopus a plan for rescuing Aegina, Zeus ordered his brother, Hades, the god of death, to drag Sisyphus to the underworld which was called *Hell*. But Sisyphus spoke so eloquently to Hades that Hades allowed him to return to the land of the living to complete an urgent task he had left undone. Once back, Sisyphus refused to return to Hell and took up again his old career of clever thievery. Fed up, Zeus sent his messenger, Hermes, to force Sisyphus back to Hell; and, he sent word to his brother to keep Sisyphus there. Hades ordered Sisyphus to push a huge boulder to the top of one of Hell's hills and leave it there to be used in a building to be constructed there. Sisyphus, by huge effort, pushed the rock up the hill using his own great strength for the task. But when the rock stood at the top of the hill, it rolled all the way back down and Sisyphus had to go down the hill and roll it up again. Again and again, for eternity, this was Sisyphus's senseless task.

The myth of Sisyphus illustrates that a myth may tell more than one truth. For instance, the myth suggests that harm can come to the person who is far too clever. Especially if the person flaunts his cleverness in the face of the gods, who, angered, can punish or even kill.

Another interpretation: the myth pictures the monotonous and backbreaking labor many men have to endure for all of their lives. Such work need not even consist of the toil and sweat of hard labor. It can be just routine itself, crushing sameness. One day after another, the same. When I think of Sisyphus I also think of the soul-killer, solitary confinement, and the deadly effect of doing anything over and over until the creativity that makes men partners with their Creator is smothered.

Perhaps you will find other truths in Sisyphus. For certain, truths can be found in all the ancient myths. The men of today, scholars and others, still mine the myths for their nuggets of wisdom.

A STORY WET AS TEARS
A Modern Fable

Remember the princess who kissed the frog so he became a prince? At first, they danced all night, and toasted each other in the morning with champagne and, always, with kisses. Perhaps it was in bed after the first year had ground around she noticed he had become cold with her. She had to sleep with heating pad and down comforter. His manner grew increasingly chilly and damp when she entered a room. He spent his time in water sports and working on his insect collection.

Then, in the third year, when she said to him one day, "My Dearest, are you taking your vitamins daily? You look quite green," he leaped away from her.

Finally, on their fifth anniversary she confronted him, "My precious, don't you love me any more?" He replied, "Rivet, Rivet."

MARGE PIERCY

Simile: Blood Brother to Metaphor

Simile is not a twin of metaphor, but they *are* blood brothers. Their family name is Comparison and, like many brothers, they look much alike. But simile is the larger of the two. Simile, in fact, is bigger by one to several words.

Let us look at these two brothers, side by side.

Metaphor: Anna snailed her way across the field.

Simile: Anna walked across the field as slowly as a snail.

Both metaphor and simile compare Anna's pace to a snail's pace but in overall size, simile is bigger by three words.

The word that most often makes simile bigger is *like*. The second most frequent is *as* or the word-form as _____ as. Third in frequency is the word *so*, or as _____ so.

These words, *as, so, like*, make metaphor and simile physically different but, more importantly, these words make them different kinds of comparisons: a metaphor is an *implicit* comparison; a simile, an *explicit* one made so by the words *as, so, like* which announce that a comparison is being made.

Take, for instance, two lines from Shakespeare's *Macbeth*. (The lines are part of an oral report to Duncan, King of Scotland, by a messenger who has run to tell the king the status of a battle raging nearby.)

Messenger:...like two tired swimmers, the armies cling together, dragging each other down.

Later the messenger says:

> Brave Macbeth carved his way forward till he faced the
> wretch, the traitor Caldwell.

In the first line, by using the word *like*, Shakespeare directs the reader
(or playgoer) to compare the behavior of desperate swimmers to what
is going on in the conflict between the army of the king and the army of
his foes.

In the second line, a metaphor-in-a-verb, *carved*, suggests, but does
not state openly, a comparison between the murderous sword play of
Macbeth as he pushes through the opposing army to confront a traitor
with the bloody assault of a butcher's knife on a carcass.

From early childhood human beings are led to make comparisons by
using simile form. (The ocean is like a huge lake.) (Your fingernails are
like Rover's claws.) Comparison is a universal way of learning and of
teaching too.

On the other hand, the reader of the second quoted line must recognize on his own that Shakespeare's metaphor-in-a-verb, *carved*, claims
that Macbeth is a butcher mauling his enemies. The claim, of course,
violates common sense. How can we live in the confusion that follows if
one thing can also *be* another thing?

The reader of the second line must perceive that the claim of identity
between unlike things points to an *implicit* comparison and that he
must discover the comparison being made for himself.

Literary critics tend to prefer metaphor to simile. They argue that
creating metaphor requires sharper intellect and keener observation.
They hold that metaphor gives greater pleasure to the reader because it
is original and striking.

To my mind, neither of the blood brothers ought to be favored over the other. I think the *aptness* of the comparison made by either metaphor or simile is what matters. The reader, I imagine, will form his own opinion as he reads the metaphors and similes in this book.

The words of comparison in the examples of simile which follow are in italic type.

I am *as* busy *as* a one-armed paper hanger with the itch.

Franklin D. Roosevelt

(Thus did this president describe his job and his life during World War II.)

As the hart panteth after the water brooks, *so* panteth my soul after thee, O God.

from the Book of Psalms

Shaking hands with President Benjamin Harrison was *like* shaking hands with a wet petunia.

Anonymous

(Probably anonymous for good reason.)

Writing with chalk on a blackboard is *like* the squeaking of brakes.

spoken by a 5th grade student.

Like a lily among brambles *so* is my darling among girls.

from the Song of Songs

Exploring the subtleties of Scholastic Philosophy is *as* profitable *as* milking a he-goat into a sieve.

Thomas More

(I've made the same judgment about some mathematical formulas and explanations of the "new" physics.)

He looked at me *as if* I was a side dish he hadn't ordered.

Ring Lardner

As flies to wanton boys are we to the gods; they kill us for their sport.

William Shakespeare in *Henry IV*

In the New Testament there is internal evidence that parts of it have proceeded from an extraordinary figure; and that other parts are of the fabric of very inferior minds. It is *as* easy to separate these parts *as* to pick out diamonds from dung hills.

Thomas Jefferson

We should be careful to get out of an experience only the wisdom that is in it—and stop there: lest we be *like* the cat that sits down on a hot stove-lid. She will never sit down on a hot stove-lid again—and that is well; but she also never will sit down on a cold one either.

Mark Twain

(During World War II Ernie Pyle was a war correspondent famous for writing stories about how the war was experienced by G. I. Joes. One day Pyle found himself at a reception for Mrs. Franklin Roosevelt who was being honored for her many trips to visit members of the armed services. As Pyle moved forward in the reception line, he wondered whether, on hearing his name, Mrs. Roosevelt might recognize him and speak to him. But when he stood before her she gave him only a smile and a handshake before turning her attention to the next in line.)

"I couldn't have been *any more* anonymous *than* if I'd been a fish in the sea." Ernie later confided to a friend.

> She's *like* the swallow that flies so high.
> She's *like* the river that never runs dry.
> She's *like* the sunshine on the ice shore.
> I love my Love.

NEWFOUNDLAND FOLK SONG

(It seems as though one simile was insufficient to describe the Love of the author of this song.)

But those who are not genuinely lovers of wisdom, in whom philosophy is no more than a superficial veneer *like* the tan men get from exposing themselves to the sun, once they see how much labor is involved…decide that the task (of becoming a true philosopher) is too hard for them and beyond their scope.

PLATO

For we, *like* children frightened
 · of the dark
Are sometimes frightened
   in the light—
Of things no more to be feared
   than fears that in the dark
Distress a child, thinking they may
   come true.
Therefore this terror and darkness
   of the mind
Must be dispersed, as is most necessary,
Not by the sun's rays, not by the bright shafts
   of day,
But by the face of nature and her laws.

LUCRETIUS

A violet by a mossy stone
Half-hidden from the eye,
Fair *as* a star when only one
Is shining in the sky.

WILLIAM WORDSWORTH

(Wordsworth wrote several poems about a young woman named Lucy who lived in an isolated place in the English countryside. Critics still disagree as to whether Lucy was flesh and blood or a figment of the poet's imagination. In this "Lucy" poem the author describes Lucy first by a metaphor. [Hint: To find the metaphor, insert Lucy is *at the head of the first line.] Then he further describes her with a simile.)*

BIRCHES

You may see their trunks arching in the woods
Years afterwards, trailing their leaves on the
   ground
Like girls on hands and knees that throw their hair
Before them over their heads to dry in the sun.

ROBERT FROST

New horizons are opened up
whenever accepted ideas
are newly understood,
whenever new relationships
are understood, whenever
a truth is stated
so emphatically that it influences future
actions and thoughts.

PETER LEVI

What Metaphor *Does*

The extant writings of the very earliest societies contain such mundane things as inventories of supplies available for sustaining a siege, lists of who owed what to some protector (taxes are nothing new), accounts of victories in battle (almost no accounts of defeats), genealogies, bits of stone engraved with a blessing or a curse. Pretty dull stuff except for the usually blood-soaked curses. But with these practicalities are also found the earliest poems and narratives (often written in poetic form) that have been discovered.

Since these so very early times there has been a vast output of poetry originating in all parts of our world. A major element in this poetry is metaphor. It, too, has appeared in each historical age and in every country. Some say metaphor is the heart of poetry—a statement that is itself a metaphor that tells the truth that metaphor is powerful, emotion-arousing language. Like poetry itself, a metaphor effects changes in those who hear or read it.

Scholars have done formal studies of how metaphor impacts on the hearts and minds of men and women. They report these principal conclusions:

— metaphor clarifies
— metaphor breaks open old ways of seeing and suggests new ways

Metaphors make the less familiar clearer by pointing to the way or ways an unfamiliar thing is like a more familiar one. Thus, metaphor is a way of clearing up perplexity about the true nature of anything.

Doubts about what some thing or concept *is* tend to make us uncomfortable or even fearful. Could it be dangerous? Will we make a costly mistake if we approach the little-known in the wrong way?

The effort to reduce perpexity about the world and ourselves has taken much of mankind's energy and time. Think, for example, of the amount of time children spend in instruction about what *is* known. Think, too, of the support society gives to the ongoing struggle to verify or discredit thinking about what reality is truly made of.

All the young are invested in identifying what things are. They are born, says William James, into a world that is to them "a big, blooming, buzzing confusion." To survive they must learn to make sense of what lies around them and within them too. One way they go about it is to notice similarities and to make something of them.

At age four my grandaughter Carrie said to me:

"A butterfly is a flying rainbow."

She had noticed similarity between multicolored things and a difference too for she made the rainbow fly before she claimed likeness.

And when he was three, my grandson Ben said:

"A cocoon is a nice warm house for a caterpillar."

At the time Ben was familiar with a nice, warm house—his home has always been one. He knew very little of a cocoon beyond appreciating that "a worm is in it and the worm will grow up to be a butterfly." He recognized that the cocoon sheltering the worm was like the home that shelters him. By noting a similarity, he gained a deeper understanding of how the world works.

For adults who live in an environment of concepts and ideas, as well as physical things, the most frequent use of metaphor is to clarify abstractions by using terms that describe familiar relationships in the physical and social worlds. An example is, "This city is a jungle." Whoever makes this statement tells the hearer of it how he perceives life in his city. From the metaphor, the hearer can surmise that whoever spoke of his city in this way, finds in it a dog-eat-dog mentality; he is afraid of its threatening nature, fearful of its inhabitants who are strange to him. By its nature the metaphor conveys information about the speaker. Compare this to the response to the question, "How is it for you in Peoria?" and the answer, "Well, it's OK sometimes but the people aren't friendly, and…, and…, and…

In this latter kind of description we find primarily a list with no overall summary of the person's relation to his city. But in the metaphor we find a statement that sums up and illumines his attitude and feelings toward the city. From the metaphor we gather important truths about this man. The metaphor opens the way, or, rather, *is* the way to this deeper understanding. Another way that metaphor contributes to valid understanding is that it questions assumptions that have become solidified, ones that are no longer questioned.

Suppose, for instance, that you are sure that to be sorrowful is regrettable but it is an emotion that will pass with time. It has, therefore, no great significance. Then (supposing again) you come across this simile: Sorrow is to the soul what the worm is to the wood. If you consider this expression with care you will realize that it contradicts, or at least offers a modification of your long-held view on the significance of sorrow. If woe acts on the person feeling it as a worm acts on wood, woe has a hidden and important and permanent influence on personality. You may test out whether the metaphor tells a truth either through a more open-minded approach to your own experience or by observing another's sorrow in an unprejudiced way without the distorting mask of established ideas.

This discussion has not named everything metaphor can do. It has pointed to what many believe are important capabilities of metaphor. But there is another route to understanding the effects of metaphor.

This is the opportunity to observe within yourself what you feel, and what you come to know, as you read and think about the many metaphors this book puts before you.

A radiant source of wisdom.
A link between the human and divine.
These works are rare, blessed gems.

LARRY DOSSEY

Metaphors of the Spirit

The world of spirit is an intangible realm, not made of physical entities, not limited to what is possible in the physical world where nothing happens outside of space and time. Many believe that this spiritual world exists and can influence our existence in the physical world. There has been an almost universal desire to find out about the spiritual realm and to talk to one another about our discoveries. One great difficulty, however, is the lack of words adequate to describing spiritual entities and how they function.

Metaphor has served over centuries as the best way, the way that comes closest, to describing man's experiences with the manifestations of spirit. These metaphors compare familiar objects, and happenings within the physical world of everyday to their less familiar counterparts within the compass of the spiritual. These metaphors have been spoken or written by wise men and women, persons in crisis, those suffering, those experiencing exalted states. They have come too from philosopers, cynics, and proponents of one religion or another or no religion at all. Surprisingly, they seldom come from theologians. As a matter of fact, metaphorical description of the concepts and spiritual figures of organized religions very often are expressed in abstractions—by theologians. Contrast, for example, the metaphorical *God is love* with the abstractions that have been written about *The Nature of the Deity*.

Children, too, say the darndest things in metaphor about the non-physical—especially before they have been led to accept that black *cannot* be white. Here is a metaphor I heard my five-year-old granddaughter say about a month ago.

"That's what life is all about, isn't it—playing the game you
want to play?"

Carrie Pinkard

Composed at one time or another, there are many, many metaphors
describing aspects of the spiritual world. For this book I chose
metaphors and similes about the cosmos, God, man, I-thou, life and
death, love, passion, soul, spirit, truth, and wisdom. In the pages that
follow, descriptions of spiritual entities in terms of concrete things and
attitudes that most of us have experienced appear. They are drawn from
various times and societies and were made by a large variety of persons.

Cosmos

This we know. All things are connected like blood which unites one family. All things are connected. Whatever befalls the earth befalls the sons of the earth. Man did not weave the web of life: he is merely a strand in it. Whatever he does to the web he does to himself.

CHIEF SEATTLE OF THE DWANISH TRIBE OF AMERICAN INDIANS

Regard this phantom world as a star at dawn, a bubble in a stream, a flash of lightning in a summer cloud, a flickering lamp—a phantom—and a dream.

THE BUDDHA

The world remains the world it was thousands of years ago; that is, the spouse of the devil.

MARTIN LUTHER

There is in this universe a Stair, or manifest Scale of creatures, rising not disorderly, or in confusion, but with a comely method and proportion.

SIR THOMAS BROWNE

They (American Indians) have what the world has lost: the ancient reverence and passions for the earth and its web of life. Since before the Stone Age they have tended that passion as a central, sacred fire. It should be our long hope to renew it in us all.

JOHN COLLIER

(from an address by Collier given when he was United States Commissioner of Indian affairs)

The Earth, sayeth thou?
The Human Race?
By Me created?
Nay: I have no remembrance of such place:
Such world I fashioned not.

THOMAS HARDY

Earth's crammed with heaven, and every common bush afire with God.

ELIZABETH BARRETT BROWNING

I (God) flame above the beauty of fields; I shine in the waters; in the suns, in the moon and the stars I burn. And by means of the airy wind, I stir everything into quickness.... For the air lives in its green power and its blossoming; the waters flow as if they were alive. Even the sun is alive in its own light; and when the moon is on the point of disappearing, it is kindled by the sun so that it lives, as it were, afresh.

HILDEGARDE OF BINGEN

(Hildegarde was a nun in medieval times. She was celebrated as a visionary)

I believe in the God who reveals himself in the orderly harmony of what exists.... it is enough for me to contemplate the mystery of conscious life perpetuating itself through all eternity, to reflect upon the marvelous structure of the universe we dimly perceive, and to try humbly to comprehend even an infinitesimal part of the intelligence manifested in nature.

ALBERT EINSTEIN

All are part of one stupendous whole. Whose body nature is, and God the soul.

ALEXANDER POPE

> If your heart is without stormy waves,
> Everywhere are blue mountains and green trees.
> If our real nature is creative like nature itself,
> Wherever we may be
> We see that all things are free
> Like sporting fishes and circling kites.

ZEN POEM

I swear the earth shall surely
    be complete to him or her
    who shall be complete.
The earth remains jagged and broken
    only to him or her
    who remains jagged or broken.

Walt Whitman

One particle of dust is raised, and the great earth lies therein;
One flower blooms, and the universe rises with it.

Yuan-Wu

The universe is made up of stories, not atoms.

Muriel Ruckeyser

Observers are not detached from reality. In the new way of looking at it, the new physics, the observer and the observed are tangled together in an inextricable way. Everything is folded together into a unity. We really do seem to play a fundamental role in the working of nature…(so) that my individual life has more purpose. It's actually interwoven into the nature of reality in a very fundamental way. So in some sense we're not just a trivial add-on to the universe, not like extras that have stumbled onto the great cosmic set just by accident—we're truly written into the script, we're truly meant to be here.

Paul Davies

WARTY BLIGGENS THE TOAD

i met a toad
the other day by the name
of warty bliggens
he was sitting under
a toadstool
feeling contented
he explained that when the cosmos
was created
that toadstool was especially
planned for his personal
shelter from sun and rain
thought out and prepared
for him

do not tell me
said warty bliggens
that there is not a purpose
in the universe
the thought is blasphemy

a little more
conversation revealed
that warty bliggens
considers himself to be
the center of the said
universe
the earth exists
to grow toadstools for him
to sit under
the sun to give him light

by day and the moon
and the wheeling constellations
to make beautiful
the night for the sake of
warty bliggens

to what act of yours
do you impute
this interest on the part
of the creator
of the universe
i asked him
why is that you
are so greatly favored

ask rather
said warty bliggens
what the universe
has done to deserve me
if i were a
human being i would
not laugh
too complacently
at poor warty bliggens
for similar
absurdities
have only too often
lodged in the crinkles
of the human cerebrum

Don Marquis

(Marquis for a very long time, was a columnist for a newspaper. One day his column changed from presenting his own political views to a paper he found in his typewriter one morning. Eventually he came to know that the paper had been typed by Archy, a cockroach with literary ambition and philosophical outlook who lived in his office. As far as we know Archy was not paid for his poems but he should have been —he had to type by hitting each key with his head but he could not manage the capitalization or question mark or period keys. Hence his poems are without these amenities. If you want to read more of Archy's work, you can find it in a book titled Archy and Mehitabel.*)*

Many-named God

In God all that is, is God.
In him the smallest creature of earth and sea
is worth no atom less
than you or me.

ANGELUS SILESIUS

There is one God—supreme among gods and men—who is like mortals in neither body nor mind.

XENAPHANES

It's name is Public Opinion. It is held in reverence. It settles everything. Some think it is the voice of God.

MARK TWAIN

What is purity of the heart? If we compare God to sunlight, we can say that the heart is like a window. Cravings, aversions, fixed judgments, concepts, beliefs—all forms of selfishness or self-protection are, when we cling to them, like dirt on a window pane. The thicker the dirt, the more opaque the window. When there is no dirt, the window is by its own nature perfectly transparent, and the light can stream through it without hindrance.

STEPHEN MITCHELL

Cast all your cares on God; that anchor holds.

ALFRED LORD TENNYSON

And that inverted bowl we call the sky, Whereunder crawling coop't we live and die. Lift not thy hand to it for help—for it Rolls impatiently on as thou or I.

OMAR KHAYYAM

Mightier than the crash of a thunderstorm, mightier that the roar of the sea, is God's voice silently speaking in the depths of the listening heart.

PSALM 93

The words of the Lord are pure words as silver tried in a furnace of earth, purified seven times.

PSALM 12

Thou hast put gladness in my heart; yea more than when their corn and wine and oil increase.

PSALM 4

When you reach the path,
you wander in the world
with the precious Buddha
Completely wrapped up inside
As in a bundle of rags.
    you have this precious Buddha.
    Unwrap it quickly !

SUTRA OF THE HOLY BUDDHA

(Although the Buddha is not regarded as a God, his teachings are treasured as highest wisdom)

As you can ascend to the top of the house by means of a ladder or a bamboo stick or a staircase or a rope, so divers are the ways and means to approach God. Different creeds are but different paths to reach the almighty.

SRI RAMAS KRISHNA

As truly as God is our father, so truly is God our Mother, and revealed that in everything, and especially in these sweet words where he says: " I am he."—that is to say: I am he, the power and greatness of fatherhood: I am he, the wisdom and the lovingness of motherhood.

JULIAN OF NORWICH

(Julian was an anchoress [something like a lay hermit] and counselor to noblemen and peasants in 15th century England.)

The Tao is well-used—
used, but never used up.
filled with infinite posssibilities.

LAO-TZU

God's grace is the beginning, the middle, and the end. When you pray for God's grace, you are like someone standing knee-deep in water and yet saying that someone in water feels thirsty, or that a fish in water feels thirsty, or that water feels thirsty.

ROMANA MAHARSKI

For God has hidden my way
    and put hedges across my path.
I sit and gnaw on my grief;
    my groans pour out like water.
My worst fears have happened,
    my nightmares have come to life.

JOB

You (the Lord) keep count of my wanderings, put
    my tears into your flask.

PSALM 56

The doctrine of some churches, such as that God took upon himself human nature, I have expressly said that I do not understand…this seems to me no less absurd than would a statement that a circle had taken on itself the nature of a square.

GHANDI

Julia Ward Howe, one day, was talking to Charles Sumner, a distinguished Senator from Massachusetts. She asked him to interest himself in the case of a person who needed some help. The Senator answered, " Julia, I've become so busy I can no longer concern myself with an individual." Julia replied, "Charles, that is quite remarkable. Even God hasn't reached that state yet."

RALPH SOCKMAN

Our faith may be encapsulated in simple stark statements like "God is love." but its implications burst, like delayed fireworks, over the long days and fast years of our lives.

JOHN SHEA

Neither a fixed abode nor a farm that is thine alone, nor any function peculiar to thyself have I given thee, Adam, to the end that according to thy judgment, thou mayest have and possess what abode, what farm, and what functions thou thyself shalt desire. The nature of all other beings is limited and constrained within the bounds of laws prescribed by Us. Thou, constrained by no limits, in accord with thine own free will, in whose hand we have placed thee, shalt ordain for thyself, the limits of thy nature. We have set thee at the world's center that thou mayest from thence more easily observe whatever is in the world. We have made thee neither of heaven nor of earth, neither mortal nor immortal, so that with freedom of choice, as though the maker and molder of thyself, thou mayest fashion thyself in whatever shape thou shalt prefer. Thou shalt have the power to degenerate into the lower forms of life which are brutish. Thou shalt have the power out of the soul's judgment, to be reborn into the higher forms which are divine.

GIOVANNI PICO DELLA MIRANDOLA

Love beauty; it is the shadow of God on the universe.

GABRIELLA MISTRAL

Christ and his prophets and apostles are not miracle-mongers.

WILLIAM BLAKE

As flies to wanton boys are we to the gods. They kill us for their sport.

WILLIAM SHAKESPEARE

God gives every bird its food but he doesn't throw it in the nest.

JOSHUA HOLLAND

The God that holds you over the pit of hell, much as one holds a spider or some loathsome insect over the fire, abhors you.... His wrath toward you burns like fire...you are ten thousand times more abominable in his eyes as the most hateful and venomous serpent is in ours. O sinner! Consider the fearful danger you are in. 'Tis a great furnace of wrath, a wide and bottomless pit,' and...you hang by a slender thread, with the flames of divine wrath flashing about it and burning it asunder...It is everlasting wrath. It would be dreadful to suffer this fierceness and wrath of Almighty God one moment; but you must suffer it to all eternity; there will be no end to this exquisite, horrible misery.

JONATHON EDWARDS

(Edwards was a Puritan preacher in the 1700's to a Puritan colony in Massachusetts. He was famous for his terrifying sermons on hell and damnation. The title of the sermon reproduced here is Sinners in the Hands of an Angry God. *It was reported that during this sermon women in the church wept and fainted. If men didn't, I surmise they just didn't get it.)*

God—
The Holy, the Peaceful, the Faithful, the Guardian over his servants, the Shelter of the orphan, the guide of the evening, the Deliverer from every affliction, the gracious, the healer, the Near of Hand, the Compassionate, the Merciful, the Very-forgiving, whose love for man is more tender than that of the mother-bird for her young.

THE KORAN

The Gods, by right of Nature, must possess an Everlasting Age of Perfect Peace. Far off, removed from us and our affairs, neither approached by Dangers or by Cares; rich in

themselves, to whom we cannot add; Not pleased by Good
Deeds; nor provoked by Bad.

LUCRETIUS

When goodness grows weak,
When evil increases,
I (God) make myself a body.
In every age I come back
To deliver the holy,
To destroy the sin of the sinner,
To establish the righteous.

BHAGAVAD—GITA

A mighty fortress is our God
A bulwark never failing
Our helper he amid the flood
Of mortal ills prevailing:

MARTIN LUTHER

I (God) led them with cords of human kindness,
 with bands of love
I was to them like those
 who lift infants to their cheeks.

HOSEA

I (God) am death, the shatterer of worlds.

BHAGAVAD GITA

CAROLYN PINKARD

As our planet takes action to cast out its manmade poisons and heal its man-caused wounds, many human inhabitants will no doubt give way to fear. Many will cling to seemingly powerful we're-God's-chosen-people religions, hoping that by doing so they will be saved from the wrath of a Vengeful God (not recognizing that the approaching "vengeance" will in reality be man's own actions coming back at him—and not recognizing that the Infinite Universal Power is far more than the narrow-minded gatekeeper of an exclusive Spiritual Country Club.)

BENJAMIN HOFF

He does not care; so I say,
   he murders both the pure and the wicked.
When the plague brings sudden death
   he laughs at the anguish of the innocent.
He hands the earth to the wicked
   and blindfolds its judges' eyes.
Who does it, if not He?

JOB

God does not play dice with the universe.

ALBERT EINSTEIN

Oh Thou, who man of baser earth did make; And who with Eden did devise the snake; For all the sin wherewith the face of man is blackened, man's forgiveness give-and-take.

OMAR KHAYYAM

DIALOGUE

God to Any Man: Will you remember me in a year?
Man: Of course.
God: In a month?
Man: Of course
God: In a week?
Man: Of course
God: In an hour?
Man: Of course.
God: In a minute?
Man: Of course.
God: In a second?
Man: Of course.
God: Knock Knock.
Man: Who's there?
God: See, you've forgotten me already!

ANONYMOUS

(There is no metaphor in Dialogue but I have included it because I like it a lot and because reaction to it, like the usual reaction to metaphor, is a startle followed by a wry acknowledgment that there is truth in it. Dialogue was brought to my attention by a friend and I want, again, to thank him.)

Man

A little flesh, a little breath, and reason to rule all—that is myself.

Marcus Aurelius

For every species of beast and bird, of reptile and sea creature, can be tamed and has been tamed by the human species; but no one can tame the tongue—a restless evil, full of deadly poison.

James, New Testament Book

We are the only eyes, mouth, hands, feet and heart that Christ has on earth.

Teresa of Avila

There is an admantine Buddha-nature within the bodies of sentient beings. Like the sun, it is essentially bright, perfect, and complete. Although vast and limitless, it is covered by the layered clouds of the five skandas (body, perception, conception, volition, and consciousness). Like a lamp inside a jar, its light cannot shine.

HUNG-JEN

Show me a man who isn't a slave; one is a slave to sex, another to money, another to ambition; all are slaves to hope and fear...and there's no state of slavery more disgraceful than one which is self-imposed.

SENECA

What's more, mind and body are born together, and grow old and weak together, For as babies toddle about with bodies soft and tender, so their minds are wobbly too. But when the trunk grows ripe with strength of adulthood, the mind is better endowed, the reason stronger, And at last when the might of age has crushed the body, and the limbs have fallen, strengthless, beaten down, then the native talent hobbles, the tongue wanders...

LUCRETIUS

(I have to say that Lucretius is wrong about the minds of babies. Their minds are not wobbly but miraculous.)

Man's imagination is his preview of coming attractions.

ALBERT EINSTEIN

No man is an island, entire of itself; every man is a piece of the continent, a part of the main.

JOHN DONNE

Man who is born of woman—how few and harsh
  are his days!
Like a flower he blooms and withers; like a shadow
  he fades in the dark.
He falls apart like a wine skin, like a garment
  chewed by moths.

Job

We follow our futile aims as we blow out a soap bubble, as long and as large as possible, although we know perfectly well it will burst.

Arthur Schopenhauer

Man postpones or remembers; he does not live in the present. We are trapped in time in that we either postpone or remember. We are constantly thinking either of what has come or what is to come. Man either laments the past or, heedless of the riches that surround him, stands on tiptoes to see the future.

Ralph Waldo Emerson

And man that strives to touch a star oft stumbles at a straw.

Edmund Spencer

I say again that this is most true, and all history bears witness to it, that men may second Fortune, but they cannot thwart her—they may weave her web, but they cannot break it.

Machiavelli

O Lord, thou art our father; we are the clay, and thou
our potter; and we are all the work of thy hand.

Isaiah

The greatest crimes are caused by surfeit, not by want. Men
do not become tyrants so as not to suffer cold.

Aristotle

Our plans miscarry because they have no aim. When a man
does not know what harbor he is making for, no wind is the
right wind.

Seneca

All that we are is the result of what we have thought; it is
founded on our thoughts, it is made up of our thoughts. If a
man speaks or acts with an evil thought, pain follows him, as
the wheel follows the foot of the ox that draws the
carriage...if a man speaks or acts with a pure thought,
happiness follows him, like a shadow that never leaves him.

Buddhist Ethical Teaching

None came into this world with a saddle on his back, neither
any booted and spurred to ride him.

Richard Rumbold, a Puritan minister

*(Richard Rumbold made this metaphor claiming his right to independent thought
from the scaffold just before he was hanged for heresy)*

I have discovered that all human evil comes from this—
man's being unable to sit still in a room.

Pascal

Everything is good when it leaves the hands of the Creator;
everything degenerates in the hands of man.

Rousseau

Happy the people whose annals are boring to read.

Montesquieu

Of course there is evil. You need to go no further back than
Hitler and Hiroshima to see concrete examples of it. Even
today, examples abound: the lunacy of terrorism; all kinds of
violence, especially against children, women, minorities and
dissenters; political torture; exploitation of the poor. All
around us is the reality of evil in its stark and effective
horror, gnawing away at everything that is good and noble
and decent in the world. Every day we see clearly the awful
toll that humanity is capable of exacting against itself. But it
is too easy to blame it all on Satan; we cannot excuse
ourselves by protesting, "The devil made me do it." We have
met the enemy and he is us.

Donald Spoto

To bless whatever there is, and for no other reason but simply
because it is, that is what we are made for as human beings.

David Stendl-Rast

Man's task is to make himself a work of art.

HENRY MILLER

I met a fellow in Key West (undoubtedly our most laid-back American community). His name was Clyde. Clyde says human beings were not made to labor from dawn to dusk. Human beings were just intended to be on this earth to enjoy themselves a bit. It's a philosophy you don't hear much in this intense, work-oriented society of ours. But to the extent you can survive without working from dawn to dusk, I've about decided Clyde is right.

CHARLES KURALT

Hamlet: (Man is) infinite in faculties, in apprehension how like a God.

WILLIAM SHAKESPEARE

A man is called silly by a god just as a child is by a man.

HERACLITUS

Space ails us Moderns;
   we are sick with space.
Its contemplation makes us out as small
   as a brief epidemic of microbes
That in a good glass may
   be seen to crawl,
The patina of this least of globes.

ROBERT FROST

. . .being human does not unfold automatically as the oak tree does from the acorn. For an intrinsic and inseparable element in being human is self-consciousness. Man is the being who has to be aware of himself, be responsible for himself, if he is to become himself. He is also that being who knows that at some future moment, he will not be; he is the being who is always in relationship with non-being, death. And he not only knows he will sometime not be, but he can, by his own choices, slough off and forfeit his being. "To be or not to be," is not a choice one makes once and for all at the point of considering suicide, it reflects a choice made at every instant.

ROLLO MAY

The tragedy of a man's life is what dies inside of him while he lives.

HENRY DAVID THOREAU

Compared to what we ought to be, we are half awake.

WILLIAM JAMES

Most people die with their music still locked up inside them.

BENJAMIN DISRAELI

A child-like man is not a man whose development has been arrested; on the contrary, he is a man who has given himself a chance of continuing to develop long after most adults have muffled themselves in the cocoon of habit and convention.

ALDOUS HUXLEY

We are in the grips of scientific materialism, caught in the vicious circle where our society today seems to depend on regimentation and weapons which will ruin us tomorrow.

CHARLES LINDBERGH

A man may fulfill the object of his existence by asking a question he cannot answer, and attempting a task he cannot achieve.

OLIVER WENDELL HOLMES

Men strain at gnats and swallow camels.

ANONYMOUS

Tien and Tao, Brahman, God and Allah all carry the signature of *ens perfectissium*-perfect being. This is reflected in estimates of the human self for in the way that the world's unity implies that selves belong to the world, its worth implies that they share in the world's exalted stature. The sheer immensity of the human self as envisioned by the world's religions is awesome. Atman and Buddha nature come immediately to mind, and we remember the rabbis' angels who precede human beings crying, "Make way for the image of God."

HUSTON SMITH

I-Thou

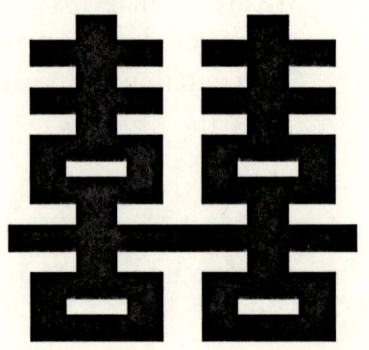

Heaven is the father and earth
   the mother of all men.
Therefore, all men are brothers and
   should dwell together as such.
By so living the country will be free
   from hate and sorrow.

AN ORACLE OF THE SHINTO GOD, ATSUTA

(The date of composition is unknown but scholars agree that this oracle is very, very ancient.)

The master is available to all people and doesn't reject anyone. What is a good man but a bad man's teacher? What is a bad man but a good man's job? If you don't understand this, you will get lost however intelligent you are. It is the great secret.

TAO TE CHING

The true opposite of love is not hate but indifference. Hate, bad as it is, at least treats the neighbor as a thou, whereas indifference turns the neighbor into a thing.

Joseph Fletcher

Our world is a battlefield of individuals and groups. But reality also is the power of reconciliation whose work is wholeness and whose name is love.

Paul Tillich

Whosoever hateth his brother is a murderer.

I John

I have given you as a light to the nations
    to open the eyes that are blind,
to bring out the prisoners from the dungeon,
    from the prison those who sit in darkness.

Isaiah

Why beholdest thou the mote that is in thy
    brother's eye but considerest not the beam that
    is in thine own eye?

Jesus of Nazareth

This is my way.
What is your way?
The way doesn't exist.

Friedrich Nietzsche

Chao-chou asked a traveling monk, "Have you ever been here before?" The monk replied yes and Chao-chou said, "Have a cup of tea." Then Chao-chou asked another visiting monk, "Have you ever been here before?" The monk answered no, and Chao-chou said, "Have a cup of tea." Then an attendant monk asked Chao-chou, "Why do you say 'Have a cup of tea' to both the monk who had been here before and the monk who hadn't?" Chao-chou called the attendant's name. The attendant replied, "Yes sir?" Choa-chou said, "Have a cup of tea."

ZEN KOAN

Snowflakes are one of nature's most fragile things, but just look what they can do when they stick together.

VERNA KELLEY

The injuries we do and those we suffer are seldom weighed in the same scales.

AESOP

Every man has leaned upon the past. Every liberty we enjoy has been bought at incredible cost. There is not a privilege or an opportunity that is not the product of other men's labors. We drink every day from wells we have not dug.

THOMAS GIBBS

Only in relationships can you know yourself, not in abstractions, and certainly not in isolation. The movement of behavior is the sure guide to yourself. It's the mirror of your consciousness; this mirror will reveal its content, the images, the attachments, the fears, the loneliness, the joy and sorrow.

J. KRISHNAMURTI

Always do right. This will gratify some people and astonish the rest.

MARK TWAIN

(I couldn't resist this non-metaphor.)

Strengthen other men and you will be strengthened.

CONFUCIUS

(This non-metaphor was equally compelling.)

May I be a balm to the sick, their healer and servitor until sickness come never again; may I quench with rains of food and drink the anguish of hunger and thirst. May I be in the famine of age's end drink and meat; may I become an unfailing store for the poor and serve them with manifold things for their need. My own being and my pleasures, all my righteousness in the past, present and future, I surrender indifferently, that all creatures win through to their end.

SHANTIDEVA

And whosoever of you will be the chiefest shall be the servant of all.

JESUS OF NAZARETH

How a minority
Reaching majority
Seizing authority
Hates a minority

L. H. ROBBINS

...the man who claims to love the Lord but is angry with his neighbor is like a man who dreams he is running.

JOHN CLIMACUS

If you live in the river you should make friends with the crocodiles.

PUNJABI PROVERB

Fill your bowl to the brim and it will spill. Chase after money and security and your heart will never unclench. Care about people's approval and you will be their prisoner.

LAO-TZU

A friend is a present you give yourself.

ROBERT LOUIS STEVENSON

May the time not be distant, O God, when corruption and evil shall give way to purity and goodness, when superstition shall no longer enslave the mind, nor idolatry blind the eye. O may all created in thine image recognize that they are brethren, so that, one in spirit and one in fellowship, they may be forever united before Thee.

FROM THE MORNING SERVICE FOR THE NEW YEAR
IN THE UNION PRAYERBOOK FOR JEWISH WORSHIP

This is the place where we must sever

You go thousands of miles, my friend

Once, forever.

Like a floating cloud we drift apart.

The sunset lingers

Like the feelings of my heart.

A CHINESE POET OF LONG AGO

For I was hungry and you gave me food,
I was thirsty and you gave me drink,
I was a stranger and you came to me.
Lord, when did we see thee hungry
And feed thee? Or thirsty and give Thee drink?

And when did we see thee a stranger
  and welcome thee?
  Or naked and clothe thee?
  And when did we see thee sick
  Or in prison and visit thee?

Truly, I say to you,
As you did it to one of these brethren,
You did it to me.

MATTHEW 25

(the speakers in the passage are alternately Jesus and his disciples.)

Really
I seem to be shy to some friends I know,
  I seem to be.
Really, I'm not shy, really.
To the students in my class,
  I seem to be kind of dumb.
  I seem to be.
But really I'm kind of smart, really.
To other people I seem to be a stranger.
  I seem to be.
But really, I'm their sister, really.

POEM BY A FOURTH GRADE STUDENT

Life and Death

The true meaning of life is to plant trees under whose shade
you do not expect to sit.

'Tis all a chequer-board of nights and days
Where Destiny with men for pieces plays;
Hither and Thither moves, and mates,
And stays and one-by-one
Back in the closet lays.

OMAR KHAYYAM

Life is either a daring adventure, or nothing.

HELEN KELLER

Human Life! Its duration is momentary, its substance in
perpetual flux, its senses dim, its physical organism
perishable, its consciousness a vortex, its destiny dark, its
repute uncertain—in fact, the material element is a rolling

stream, the spiritual element, drains and vapors. Life is a war and a sojourning in a far country. What can see us through?

Marcus Aurelius

Imperial Caesar, dead and turned to clay,
Might stop a hole to keep the wind away.

William Shakespeare

The Master holds nothing back
from life;
Therefore he is ready for death
As a man is ready for sleep
after a good day's work.

Lao-Tzu

Life can be pulled by goals just as surely as it can be pushed by drives.

Victor Frankl

Go to your rest with good grace, as an olive falls in its season, with a blessing for the earth that bore it and a thanksgiving to the tree that gave it life.

Marcus Aurelius

One thinks, schemes, plans,
   contrives projects,
Aware that he is mental;
But still, a large part of
   one's life
Is just coincidental.

LEVERETT LYON

Life cannot wait until the sciences may have explained the universe scientifically. We cannot put off living until we are ready. The most salient characteristic of life is its coerciveness: it is always urgent, "here and now" without any postponement. Life is fired at us point-blank.

AUTHOR UNKNOWN

Life is not a spectacle or a feast; it is a predicament.

GEORGE SANTAYANA

Life is a voyage that's homeward bound.

HERMAN MELVILLE

Life is like standing at the top of a mountain in wind and snow. There are paths that lead down: some of these will dash you over a crevice, You cant see which path to follow, but you must have the courage to move.

WILLIAM JAMES

CAROLYN PINKARD

Macbeth: Life's but a walking shadow…It is a tale told by an idiot, full of sound and fury, signifying nothing.

WILLIAM SHAKESPEARE

(These lines from the play, Macbeth, *are spoken by Macbeth immediately after he is informed of the death of Lady Macbeth.)*

> Remember, life is a breath:
>   soon I will vanish from your sight.
> Like a cloud fading in the sky
>   man dissolves into death.
> He leaves the whole world behind him
> and never comes home again.

JOB

The aim of Zen is to focus the attention on reality itself, instead of our intellectual and emotional reactions to reality—reality being the ever-changing, ever growing, indefinable something known as "life" which will never stop for a moment for us to fit it satisfactorily into any rigid system of pigeonholes and ideas.

ALAN WATTS

Consider too the blind lust for status that drives pathetic men to overstep the bounds of right and may even turn them into accomplices or instruments of crime, struggling night and day with unstinted effort to scale the pinnacles of wealth. These are the running sores of life.

LUCRETIUS

Life is too short to be little.

BENJAMIN DISRAELI

I have spent most of my life in the basement but if I had it to live over I would live in the upper stories.

SIGMUND FREUD

(The quote that follows is from the play Our Town. *The scene is the cemetery of a small town in New Hamshire. The characters are the dead who are buried there. They have the capacity to speak to each other but cannot speak to the live persons who visit the cemetery. The speaker here is Simon Stinson, a man long dead. He speaks to Emily, a young woman who died very recently. She has been granted a wish to observe one day of her life. She chose to observe her 12th birthday. Very upset, she has returned to her grave.)*

Simon Stinson: (speaking to Emily) Yes, now you know! Now you know! That's what it was like to be alive. To move about in a cloud of ignorance, to go up and down trampling on feelings of those about you. To spend and waste time as though you had a million years. To be always at the mercy of one self-centered passion or another. Now you know—that's the happy existence you want to go back to. Ignorance and blindness.

THORNTON WILDER

Life is a succession of lessons which must be lived in order to be understood.

RALPH WALDO EMERSON

Life can only be understood backwards but it must be lived forwards.

HEGEL

Life and death are not biological states, but states of being, of relating to the world. Life means constant change, constant birth. Death means cessation of growth, ossification, repetition. The unhappy fate of many is that they do not make the choice. They are neither alive nor dead. Life becomes a burden, an aimless enterprise, and busyness is the means to protect one from the torture in the land of shadows.

ERICH FROMM

The Body
of
Benjamin Franklin, Printer
Like the cover of an old book
Its contents torn out
and stripped of its lettering and gilding
Lies here, food for worms
For it will (as he believes) appear once
more
In a new
and more beautiful Edition
Corrected and Amended
by the Author

(Benjamin Franklin himself wrote this epitaph. As he wished, it appears on his gravestone.)

Love

Love is intensity, that second in which the doors of time and space open just a crack.

Octavio Paz

Take away love and our earth is a tomb.

Robert Browning

The best way to obtain true happiness is, without any rules, to throw out from oneself on all sides, like a spider, an adhesive web of love to catch in it all that comes; an old woman, a child, a girl, or a policeman.

Leo Tolstoy in his Diary

Love doesn't make the world go round. Love is what makes the ride worthwhile.

Franklin P. Jones

There is a land of the living
　and a land of the dead,
　and the bridge is love,
The only survival, the only meaning.

THORNTON WILDER

A good heart, Kate, is the sun and the moon; or rather, the sun, and not the moon, for it shines bright and never changes, but keeps his course, truly.

WILLIAM SHAKESPEARE

Some of us have survived this bloodiest of centuries, but if its ordeals are to be birth pangs rather than death throes, the century's scientific advances must be matched by comparable advances in human relations. Those who listen work for peace, a peace built not on ecclesiastical or political hegemonies but on understanding and mutual concern. For understanding, at least in realms as inherently noble as the great faiths of humankind, brings respect; and respect prepares the way for a higher power, love—the only power that can quench the flames of fear, suspicion and prejudice, and provide the means by which the people of this small but precious earth can become one to one another.

HUSTON SMITH

Love does not cause suffering;
what causes it is the sense of ownership,
which is love's opposite.

ANTOINE DE SAINT-EXUPERY

Work is love made visible.

KAHIL GIBRAN

I will stand and sing out
   the power of your forgiveness
I will teach your love to the ignorant,
   the lost will find their way home.

PSALM 51

If you the sea held, I would follow you, my wife until me also
the sea held.

OVID

MY FATHER

I remember him
   like God in my heart.
I remember him in my heart
   like strawberry ice cream and bananas
   when I was a little kid.
But the most I remember
   is his love
   as big as Texas
When I was born.

POEM WRITTEN BY A 5TH GRADE STUDENT

CAROLYN PINKARD

Love shook my heart as a gale
Falls upon trees on a mountainside.

SAPPHO

Oh life is a glorious cycle of song
A medley of extemporanea
And love is a thing that can never go wrong
And I am Marie of Rumania

DOROTHY PARKER

They (the "good" man and the "good" woman) think they love God! It is only his old clothes, of which they make scarecrows for the children. Where will they come nearer to God than in those very children?

HENRY DAVID THOREAU

I have seen none who love moral worth as he loves women's beauty.

CONFUCIUS

(Not a metaphor but worth thinking about.)

...but I look on thee...on thee
Beholding, besides love, the end of love,
Hearing oblivion beyond memory;
As one who sits and gazes from above
Over the rivers to the bitter sea.

ELIZABETH BARRETT BROWNING

…for love is as fierce as death,
it's jealousy bitter as the grave.
Even its sparks are a raging fire,
or devouring flame.

FROM THE SONG OF SONGS

True life, eternal life, has been found. It is not something promised, it is already here, it is *within you* as life lived in love, in love without subtraction or exclusion, without distance.

FRIEDRICH NIETZSCHE

Love your enemies, do good to those who hate you, bless those who curse you, pray for those who abuse you. If anyone strikes you on the cheek, offer the other also; and from anyone who takes away your coat, do not withold even your shirt.

JESUS OF NAZARETH

Passion

(By passion *I refer to intense, heart-and-mind-stirring emotion.)*

> Restless man's mind is
> So strongly shaken
> In the grip of the senses.
>
> BHAGAVAD GITA

> Of course one gets bored
>   and passion cools
> But always desire begins
>   to spiral again—
> Like a horse bolting with one helpless rider
>   tugging at the reins.
>
> OVID

> Seeing's believing but feeling's the truth.
>
> THOMAS FULLER

We must picture hell as a state where everyone is perpetually concerned about his own dignity and advancement, where everyone has a grievance, and where everyone lives the deadly serious passions of envy, self-importance, and resentment...The greatest evil is not now done in those sordid "dens of crime" that Dickens loved to paint. It is conceived and ordered (moved, seconded, carried and minuted) in clean, carpeted, warmed and well-lighted offices by quiet men with white collars and cut fingernails and smooth-shaven cheeks who do not need to raise their voice. Hence, my symbol for hell is the offices of a thoroughly nasty business concern.

C. S. Lewis

The basic insecurity of human existence and the driving anxiety connected with it are felt everywhere and by everyone. It is a human heritage.

Paul Tillich

Being trampled to death by geese is a slow way of dying, and letting oneself be torn and worn to death by envy also is a long-drawn-out process.

Soren Kierkegaard

Envy's a coal come hissing hot from hell.

Philip Bailey

The worldly hope men set their hearts upon
Turns ashes—or it prospers; and anon
Like snow upon the desert's dusty face
Lighting a little hour or two—is gone.

OMAR KHAYYAM

You cannot prevent the birds of sorrow from flying over your
head, but you can prevent them from building nests in your
hair.

CHINESE PROVERB

Sorrow gives me no respite,
    anguish crushes my heart.
I am like an owl in the wilderness,
    like a hawk in the desert places.
All night I lie awake,
    like a sparrow on a rooftop.
My food has all turned to ashes;
    tears are my only drink.

PSALM 102

For pain does not spring from the dust
    or sorrow sprout from the soil.

Man is the father of sorrow,
    as surely as sparks fly upward.

JOB

Pain penetrates
Me. Drop by drop.

SAPPHO

Sorrow is to the soul what the worm is to the wood.

TURKISH PROVERB

and if i ever touched a life, i hope that i know that touching
was, is, and always will be the only true revolution.

NIKKI GIOVANNI

(It is the choice of this writer to use no capital letters.)

What a new face courage puts on everything.

RALPH WALDO EMERSON

We have no greater enemy than fear. It hems us in, sucks the
joy out of life, and leaves us with disgust for ourselves.

LAURENCE BOLDT

Wrath is a passion which defiles the soul. The wise man will
avoid wrath lest he be caught in the toils of this passion as a
fly is caught in glue.

FROM A BOOK ABOUT JAINISM

Not the fastest horse can catch a word spoken in anger.

CHINESE PROVERB

The hot sun melts the snows;
When anger comes, wisdom goes.

HINDU PROVERB

To give way to wrath is to bind oneself to a master who will destroy one.

FROM THE DHAMMPODA, A SACRED BOOK OF BUDDHISM

A man that studieth revenge keeps his own wounds green which otherwise would heal and do well.

FRANCIS BACON

The mind is its own place, and itself can make a Heaven of Hell, a Hell of Heaven.

JOHN MILTON

Grief can take care of itself: but to get the full value of joy you must have someone to divide it with.

MARK TWAIN

I am free of all prejudices. I hate everyone equally.

W. C. FIELDS

Passion and faith are the songs of hallelujah land.

CALVIN PINKARD

A merry heart doeth good like a medicine.

FROM THE PSALMS

Against the assault of laughter nothing can stand.

MARK TWAIN

Dammit boss, I like you too much not to tell you. You've got everything, everything but a little madness. A man needs a little madness, otherwise he will always be afraid to cut the ropes and truly be free.

NIKOS KAZANTZAKIS IN *ZORBA THE GREEK*

Pride is a denial of God, an invention of the devil, contempt for men.

JOHN CLIMACUS

We can destroy ourselves by cynicism and delusion, just as effectively as by bombs.

KENNETH CLARK

Between these two poles…we seek to become complete: between the awesome fears that shrink us and the capacity for love that enlarges us beyond measure.

KATHLEEN NORRIS

Soul and Spirit

Out of suffering have emerged the strongest souls; the most massive characters are seared with scars.

E. H. Chapin

When my soul was embittered
   when I was pricked in heart,
I was stupid and ignorant;
   I was like a brute beast toward you.

Psalm 73

The soul knows no persons. It invites every man to expand to the full circle of the universe.

Ralph Waldo Emerson

A foolish consistency is the hobgoblin of little minds…. With consistency a great soul has simply nothing to do.

Ralph Waldo Emerson

Our demons are our own limitations which shut us off from the realization of the ubiquity of the spirit.

JOSEPH CAMPBELL

The soul-journey resembles very much the sort of adventure one encounters in folklore and myth. According to archaic view, all men have the chance to become Odysseus…

PAUL ZWEIG

Our bodily food is changed into us, but our spiritual food changes us into itself.

MEISTER ECKHART

Though thou has ever so many counselors yet do not forsake the counsel of your own soul.

JOHN RAY

God knows our secret drives and the back wards of our souls.

JOHN SHEA

You will not find the limits of the soul though you take every road, so deep is the tale of it.

HERACLITUS

Before the revelations of the soul, Time and Space and Nature shrink away.

RALPH WALDO EMERSON

Like the deer that yearns
    for running streams,
So my soul is yearning
    for you, my God.

PSALM 42

I decline to accept the end of man. I believe that man will not merely endure; he will prevail. He is immortal, not because he alone among creatures has an inexhaustible voice, but because he has a soul capable of compassion and sacrifice and endurance.

WILLIAM FAULKNER

Compassion is the strength and the soul of religion.

KATHLEEN NORRIS

The disease of contemporary man is that his soul has gone stale, he is fed up, and all about him there is a bad smell—the smell of failure. His blocked instinctual powers turn within the individual into resentment, self-hatred, hostility and aggression.

FRIEDRICH NIETZSCHE

By all means use sometimes to be alone. Salute thyself: see what thy soul doth wear.

GEORGE HERBERT

Great souls are portions of eternity.

JAMES RUSSELL LOWEL

These two wills within me, one old, one new, one the servant of the flesh, the other of the spirit, tore my soul apart.

ST. AUGUSTINE

All the things of the body are as a river and the things of the soul, a dream…

MARCUS AURELIUS

The ancient Hindu sages pondered the fact that all things—even the granite of the mountains and the mountains themselves—eventually disappear. They were struck, too, by the eternal recurrence of life—by the caterpillar that became a butterfly and the butterfly egg that became a caterpillar. Individual bits of life, the sages reasoned, must be born again and again, passing from vegetable to animal, from animal to man, from one human body to another, up the scale, down the scale. And, behind the impermanent material world, like the face behind the mask, the sages concluded, must be the invisible source of these individual bits of life and of all things—pure and unchanging spirit.

I. H. QURESHI

Truth and Wisdom

A single atom of the sweetness of wisdom in a man's heart is better than a thousand pavilions in Paradise.

Abu Yazid al-Bestami

Truth is something that works. It is a vehicle empowered to carry us to our destination.

Joyce Carol Oates

We lie in the lap of immense intelligence, which makes us receivers of its truth and organs of its activity.

Ralph Waldo Emerson

In order to swim one takes off all one's clothes—in order to aspire to the truth one must undress in a far more inward sense, divest oneself of all one's inward clothes, of thought, conceptions, selfishness, etc., before one is sufficiently naked.

Soren Kierkegaard

Zeal without wisdom is a runaway horse.

Latin proverb

All that we know is nothing, we are merely crammed wastepaper baskets, unless we are in touch with that which laughs at all our knowing.

D. H. Lawrence

I fear that as we render to our consciousness an account of our daily fortunes and behavior, we too often weave a tissue of romantic compliments and dull excuses...we all of us write such a diary in airy characters upon our brain. But the bald truth about oneself, what we are all too timid to admit when we are not too dull to see it, is what makes a man sillier and more cowardly than he need be.

Robert L. Stevenson

The best mind-altering drug is truth.

Lily Tomlin

Proceeding to the kind of people we should strive to become, we encounter the *virtues* which the wisdom traditions identify as basically three: humility, charity and veracity. Humility is not self abasement. It is the capacity to regard oneself in the company of others as one but not more than one. Charity shifts that shoe to the other foot: it is to regard one's neighbor as likewise one, as fully one as oneself. As for veracity, it extends beyond the minimum of truth-telling to sublime objectivity, the capacity to see things exactly as they are. To conform one's life to the way things are is to live authentically. The Asian religions extol these same three virtues while emphasizing the obstacles that must be overcome in acquiring them. The Buddha identified these obstacles as greed, hatred and delusion and called them the three poisons. To the degree that they are eliminated, selflessness (humility), compassion (charity), and seeing things in their suchness (veracity) replace them.

HUSTON SMITH

Every speaker has a mouth,
An arrangement rather neat.
Sometimes it's filled with wisdom,
Sometimes it's filled with feet.

ANONYMOUS

When the approach to enlightenment is like the swift thrust of a sword to the center of all things, then both worldliness and saintliness are eliminated, and the true reality is revealed.

KUEI-SHAN

A great many people think they are thinking when they are merely rearranging their prejudices.

WILLIAM JAMES

Therefore…be lamps unto yourselves. Betake yourselves to no external refuge. Hold fast as a refuge to the truth. Work out your own salvation with diligence.

THE BUDDHA

Men stumble over the truth from time to time but most pick themselves up and hurry off as if nothing happened.

WINSTON CHURCHILL

The truth is that all ideologies sooner or later get to be circumvented by cynicism and defended by hysteria, and that principle will meet you everywhere you turn in a world driven crazy by ideologies.

NORTHROP FRYE

Suddenly true reality appears like the brightness of lightning in a formerly dark place. Or, slowly, true reality appears like a landscape when the fog becomes thinner and thinner and finally disappears. New darknesses, new fogs will fall upon you; but you have experienced, at least once, the truth and the freedom given by truth. Or you may be grasped by the truth in an encounter with a piece of nature—its beauty and its transitoriness; or in a human being in friendship, in love, in difference or in hate; or in an encounter with yourself in a sudden insight into the hidden strivings of your soul. In these encounters you may meet the truth which liberates from illusions and false authorities, from enslaving anxieties, from a wrong self-rejection or a wrong self-affirmation.

PAUL TILLICH

CAROLYN PINKARD

Be as wise as serpents and innocent as doves.

JESUS OF NAZARETH

(In this saying Jesus appears to adopt the belief, already ages old in his time, that snakes are very wise. The snakes that I have seen do not, to my mind, seem wise. But have we gained by downgrading the cause of their behavior to "instinct" and finding nothing in it for us to emulate? Perhaps, like all living things the snake embodies a piece of the innate wisdom of life. At least a snake seems to know when to curl up in a sunny spot and relax completely.)

Unless it grows out of yourself no knowledge is really yours, it is only borrowed plumage.

D. T. SUZUKI

Our lives are based on what is reasonable and common sense; truth is apt to be neither.

CHRISTMAS HUMPHREYS

Many of us walk around with deeply ingrained beliefs that limit our experience. For example, we think: "You can't really do or have what you want in life." Of course, we can insist on these kinds of beliefs, select our own supportive incidents from the past, and build cases for why they are so; but this only shuts the door on new experience. As only an empty cup can be filled, so only a heart emptied of the pride of what it thinks it knows can be open to new experience and receive the gift of truth. When we embrace the humility to meet life head-on, without the baggage of what we think we know, we make room for ourselves to grow.

LAURENCE BOLDT

Looking back on the history
of mankind we see that
metaphor has been a natural—
even an essential—way of teaching.

Cleanth Brooks

How forcible are right words!

Job

Metaphor as Lesson

In the end, most metaphors proffer a lesson in the sense that if we ponder them we learn what truth they tell.

Clearly metaphor as analogy tells a story intended to be instructive. Great teachers have chosen metaphor as a teaching tool believing that a metaphor will capture the attention of a student, interest him throughout the telling, and promote retention of what has been learned. Among those who have taught by metaphor with notable success have been the poets of the Hebrew Bible, Buddha, Plato, Jesus, sages of the East, and myth-makers.

In reading this book to this point you, reader, have met a very few of all the metaphors from the unimaginably large number that have been created in a deliberate attempt to use them as teaching material. These metaphors emphasize a point of view the creator of the metaphor believes to be profound truth. Metaphors surrounded by this aura make up the chapter *Metaphor as Lesson*. They form a potpourri of convictions expressed at different times and in different places by all sorts of people.

> That's the problem with spiritual teachers. They *have* to be blabbermouths. But their words are fingers pointing at the moon; if you watch the finger, you can't see the moon.
>
> Po Chu-i

Stand up in the ways, and see, and ask for the old paths where is the good way, and walk therein.

Jeremiah

Blessed are they which do hunger and thirst after righteousness.

Jesus of Nazareth

The hardest thing to learn in life is which bridge to cross and which to burn.

David Russell

Beware lest wealth shut the door on the good life.

from the Rig Veda, a book of Hindu sacred writings

As he brews, so shall he drink.

Ben Jonson

We have no reason to harbor any mistrust against our world, for *it* is not against *us*. If it has terrors, they are *our* terrors; if it has abysses, these abysses belong to us; if there are dangers, we must try to love them. And if only we arrange our lives in accordance with the principle that we must always trust in the difficult, what now appears to us as most alien will become our most intimate and trusted experience. How could we forget those ancient myths that stand at the beginning of all races, the myths about dragons that at the last moment are transformed into princesses? Perhaps all the dragons in our lives are princesses who are only waiting to see us act, just once, with beauty and courage. Perhaps everything that frightens us is, in its deepest essence, something that wants our love.

RAINER MARIA RILKE

Laughter is the jam on the toast of life. It adds flavor, keeps it from becoming too dry, and makes it easier to swallow.

DIANE JOHNSON

Whereas gold is the kindest of all hosts when it shines in the sky; it comes an evil guest unto those that receive it in their hand.

PLUTARCH

If you don't crack the shell, you can't eat the nut.

PERSIAN PROVERB

Ring the bells that still can ring.
Forget your perfect offering.
There is a crack in everything.
That's how the light gets in.

LEONARD COHEN

For one who has conquered the mind, the mind is the best of friends. But for one who has failed to do so, his very mind will be his greatest enemy.

BHAGAVAD-GITA

I speak from experience: those who plough iniquity and sow disaster, reap just that.

JAP

Therefore whosoever heareth these sayings of mine, and doeth them, I will liken him unto a wise man, which built his house upon a rock; and the rain descended, and the floods came, and the winds blew and beat upon that house; and it fell not: for it was founded upon a rock.

JESUS OF NAZARETH

One law for the lion and the ox is oppression.

WILLIAM BLAKE

The individual piece only has meaning when it is seen as part of the whole jigsaw.

G. W. F. HEGEL

You must either conquer and rule, serve and lose, suffer or triumph, be the anvil or the hammer.

GOETHE

All changes, even the most longed for, have their melancholy, for what we leave behind us is part of ourselves; we must die to one life before we can live another.

ANATOLE FRANCE

When a man is wrapped up in himself, he makes a pretty small package.

JOHN RUSKIN

I am really mortified to be told that in the United States of America the sale of a book on religion can become a subject of criminal inquiry. Is this our freedom of religion? Are we to have a censor who shall say what books may be sold and what we may buy? Whose foot is to be the measure to which ours are all to be cut or stretched?...For God's sake, let us freely read any book on religion that we choose.

THOMAS JEFFERSON

Education is not filling a bucket but lighting a fire.

WILLIAM BUTLER YEATS

Trying to control the future is like trying to take the master carpenter's place. When you handle the master carpenter's tools, chances are that you will cut your hand.

LAO-TZU

A person's errors are his portals of discovery.

James Joyce

Look to this day
For yesterday is but a dream
And tomorrow is only a vision
But today, well lived,
Makes every yesterday a dream of happiness
And every tomorrow a vision of hope
Look well, therefore, to this day.

Sanskrit teaching

Among the worst—to be a slavedriver to yourself.

Henry David Thoreau

Find a little magic every day…especially today.

Anonymous

(Not a metaphor but close. It appeared on a birthday card I received.)

Hell has three gates: lust, anger and greed.

Bhagavad Gita

Be bold as a leopard, quick as an eagle, swift as a gazelle, and strong as a lion to do the will of your heavenly Father.

Rabbi Yehuda ben Tema

Do not criticize another until you've gone a mile in his shoes. (Then when you criticize him you will be a mile away from him and you'll have his shoes.)

AMERICAN INDIAN PROVERB

(The first sentence is the proverb. Within the parenthesis is an addition to the proverb concocted by Click and Clack, a couple of madcap auto mechanics who are hosts of a public broadcasting program.)

Obedience
bane of all genius, virtue, freedom, truth
makes slaves of men,
and of the human frame
a mechanised automaton.

PERCY B. SHELLEY

Nothing great is created suddenly: any more than a bunch of grapes or a fig.

EPICTETUS

Great things are done when men and mountains meet; this is not done by jostling in the street

WILLIAM BLAKE

Though we do not preach the doctrine,
    unasked the flowers bloom in spring;
They fall and scatter,
    They turn to dust.

IKKYU

In the archer there is a resemblance to the mature person.
When he misses the mark, he turns and seeks the reason for
his failure in himself.

Confucius

Soap and education
are not as sudden as a massacre,
but they are more deadly
in the long run.

Mark Twain

This is It
and I am It
and You are It
and He is It
and She is It
and It is It

James Broughton, a student of Zen

You must be neither on stilts nor too low.

John Dryden

Let us have wine and women,
mirth and laughter,
Sermons and soda water
the morrow.

Lord Byron

Remember that you are an actor in a play, the character of which is determined by the Playwright: if he wishes the play to be short, it is short; if long, it is long; if he wishes you to play the part of a beggar, remember to play this role adroitly; and so if your role be that of a cripple, an official or a layman. For this is your business, to play admirably the role assigned you; but the selection of that role is Another's.

EPICTETUS

The present contains all that there is. It is holy ground.

ALFRED NORTH WHITEHEAD

Spare me the din of your chanting
Let me hear none of your strumming on lyres
But let justice flow like water
And righteousness like a never-failing stream.

BOOK OF AMOS

I have good medicine but I can't take it for you.

HUANG PO, A ZEN MASTER

Drink and sing.
An inch before us is black night.

JAPANESE PROVERB

Our life is frittered away by detail. Simplify, simplify.

Henry David Thoreau

Seek not for fresher founts afar, Just drop your bucket where you are.

Sam Foss

Experience is the best of school masters, only the school fees are heavy.

Thomas Carlyle

I don't know if this is the best of times or the worst of times, but I can assure you of this: this is the only time you've got— and you can either sit on your (expletive deleted) or go out and pick a daisy.

Art Buchwald

SONG

Let's find a Way
Today
That can take us to tomorrow—
Follow that Way,
A Way like flowing water.

Let's leave
Behind
The things that do not matter,
And turn
Our lives
To a more important chapter.

Let's take the time,
Let's try to find
What real life has to offer.
And maybe then
We'll find again
What we had long forgotten.
Like a friend,
True 'til the end,
It will help us onward.

The sun is high,
The road is wide,
And it starts where we are standing.
No one knows
How far it goes,
For the road is never-ending.

It goes
Away,
Beyond what we have thought of;
It flows
Away,
Away like flowing water.

Piglet, friend of Pooh

Piglet made up this song to celebrate what he had learned from many experiences he had as he grew up in the 100-acre wood. Benjamin Hoff wrote down the song and put it into a book he wrote titled The Te of Piglet.

Afterword

Sometimes I play around with creating "what if" scenarios in my mind. What if, for instance, our world lacked the wheel, or the printing press, or ships, or sunrises?

Similarly, one can imagine that language lacks metaphor. Lost to us, then, would be the lies that tell the truth which, over centuries, have taught us how to see in a different light, and so to think in new ways. Lost, too, would be the beauty of metaphorical language and the pleasure it gives us. And, consider the approach to discovering what is real that inheres in metaphor. Science, we know, informs about physical structure and function. By contrast, metaphor has the power to approach the elusive spiritual essence of things. Without the aid of metaphor we would be one-eyed in searching for inclusive knowledge and for meaning.

In his poem, *Ulysses*, the poet, Tennyson, calls the search into the nature of things an obligation of all men. Each person must undertake, he avers, to search throughout life for truth with all the passion and skill he can muster.

ULYSSES

(The poem is a monologue by Ulysses, hero of the Trojan war—now an aged king.)

> ...all experience is an arch wherethro
> gleams that untraveled world,
> Whose margin fades for ever and for ever...
> And this gray spirit (Ulysses) yearning in desire
> To follow knowledge like a sinking star,
> Beyond the utmost bound of human thought.

In this book I claim that understanding and using metaphor can help to fill the sail in ones own voyage of discovery. I hope the discussion in the book has deepened the reader's understanding of the lies that tell the truth. Nonetheless, I am sure that the metaphors that make the bulk of the book, themselves have been the best teacher. For surely metaphor, of all word-forms, speaks most eloquently for itself.

About the Author

Carolyn Pinkard was born in a small town in Vermont to Swedish immigrant parents. As a child she enjoyed hiking, skiing and making pine needle "houses" on the mountain at the back of her home. She attended the University of Vermont graduating in 1946 with a B.A. degree in English literature. After two years of experience as editor, reporter and inexperienced printer on a weekly newspaper (with a staff of one) she went to the University of Florida to study journalism. Becoming intrigued with psychology, she stayed until 1955 earning the Ph.D. in clinical psychology in that year. Since then she has devised and led a program for teaching pastoral counseling to clergy; had a private practice in psychology, and led workshops in dream analysis and hypnotic techniques in psychotherapy. For many years she was a professor of counseling at the University of South Florida. A member of Phi Beta Kappa, she also is a diplomate in clinical psychology. Now retired, she delights in sharing her love of poetry with her young grandchildren and has co-authored with them a book of poems titled *Wordplay*. She lives with her husband on a lake in a rural area near Tampa, Florida.

Printed in the United Kingdom
by Lightning Source UK Ltd.
9799800001B/96